Selected Poems

Also by Vivian Smith
The Other Meaning
An Island South
Familiar Places
Tide Country
James McAuley
Les Vigé en Australie
The Poetry of Robert Lowell
Vance and Nettie Palmer
Vance Palmer
Letters of Vance and Nettie Palmer 1915–63 (ed.)

Vivian Smith

Selected Poems

PR
9619.3
.S57
A17
1985
c.2

Publication assisted by the
Literature Board of the Australia Council,
the Federal Government's arts funding
and advisory body.

ANGUS & ROBERTSON PUBLISHERS

Unit 4, Eden Park, 31 Waterloo Road,
North Ryde, NSW, Australia 2113 and
16 Golden Square, London W1R 4BN,
United Kingdom

This book is copyright.
Apart from any fair dealing for the
purposes of private study, research,
criticism or review, as permitted
under the Copyright Act, no part may
be reproduced by any process without
written permission. Inquiries should
be addressed to the publishers.

First published in Australia
by Angus & Robertson Publishers in 1985

Copyright © Vivian Smith 1985

National Library of Australia
Cataloguing-in-publication data.

Smith, Vivian, 1933-
    Selected poems.

    ISBN 0 207 15145 8.

    I. Title.

A821'.3

Typeset in 9pt Trump Mediaeval
by Graphicraft Typesetters Ltd
Printed in Australia by
The Dominion Press–Hedges & Bell

PREFACE

This selection contains poems written between 1952 and 1983 and it is as rigorous as I have been able to make it without completely disowning the younger poet from whom my more recent work has developed. A few poems, from which I now feel a certain distance, have been included at the request or on the advice of friends. Apart from one or two details of punctuation and wording I have not tried to revise or rewrite.

Reading my poems through again to make this selection, I noticed how a group or cycle starting in one book is often completed in another — some of the lyrics in *An Island South*, for instance, continue impulses already explored in *The Other Meaning*, and the same applies to later collections. And I have become more conscious than ever of the centrality and polarity of the two places in which I have spent most of my life: Hobart and Sydney. They seem to represent the two extreme points between which my poems move.

Translation has been an important stimulus to me from the time when I first started to write poetry as an adolescent, and I have often been drawn to poets whose preoccupations and use of language are completely different from my own, but with whom I have felt some affinity. A selection of this work is included.

Vivian Smith
Sydney, 1984

ACKNOWLEDGEMENTS

Poems reprinted from *The Other Meaning* were first published by Edwards and Shaw of Sydney for the Lyre-Bird Writers and the Commonwealth Literary Fund; "Lines for Rosamond McCulloch", "View from the Domain, Hobart" and "Summer Notes" first appeared in book form in David Malouf's anthology, *Gesture of a Hand*, published by Holt, Rinehart and Winston. Acknowledgements for poems in this collection not previously published in book form are due to *Island Magazine*, *Poetry Australia* and the *Sydney Morning Herald*.

CONTENTS

From *The Other Meaning*

Bedlam Hills	3
Bird Sanctuary	4
Old Men Are Facts	5
Fishermen, Winter	6
Winter Foreshore	7
Aloes and Sea	8
Penguin	9
Fishermen, Drowned beyond the West Coast	10
Man with Greyhounds	11
This Time of Calm	12
In Summer Rain	13
Deserted Bandstand, Kingston Beach	14
Portuguese Laurel, Flowering	15
The Last Summer	16
Late Autumn Dove	17
Equinox	18
Praying Mantis	19
The Other Meaning	20
Alceste	21
The Shadow	22
Thylacine	23
These Wrens, This Wattle Tree	24
Myth	25

From *An Island South*

At an Exhibition of Historical Paintings, Hobart	29
Winter	31
Despite the Room	32
Reflections	33
Return of the Prodigal Son	34
For My Daughter	35
Absence	36
Summer Band Concert	37
Early Arrival: Sydney	38
Summer Sketches: Sydney	39
Return to Hobart	40
Philoctetes	41
Family Album	42

ix

Quiet Evening	43
Deathbed Sketch	44
Bus Ride	47
Wrong Turning	49
One Season	50
An Effect of Light	51
Dialogue	52
There Is No Sleight of Hand	53
Beyond This Point	54
For a New Year	55
Late April: Hobart	56
Warmth in July: Hobart	57

From *Familiar Places*

View from the Domain, Hobart	61
Balmoral Summer '66	62
Summer Notes	63
Postcard from the Subtropics	64
A Room in Mosman	65
Lines for Rosamond McCulloch	66
A Few Words for Maxi	67
For Edith Holmes: Tasmanian Painter	68
For Nan Chauncy: 1900–1970	69
Coins and Bricks	70
Slope with Boulders	71
Back in Hobart	72
Twenty Years of Sydney	73
Il Convento, Batignano	74
The Traveller Returns	75
The Man Fern near the Bus Stop	76

From *Tide Country* with new poems

Onion in a Jar	79
My Morning Dip	80
The Edge of Winter	81
Still Life	82
The Restorers	83
Revisiting	84
The Tower	85
Late May: Sydney	86
Looking Back	87

Dung Beetles	88
Tasmania	89
Autumn Reading	90
Convolvulus	91
At the Parrot House, Taronga Park	92
From Korea	93
Chance Meeting	94
Sparrows: Mosman	95
Poetry Reading	96
In the Colonial Museum	97
Translations and Variations	
Delie, Obiect de Plvs Havlte Vertu (1544)	98
Variations on Garnier's *Perpetuum Mobile*	99
Summer Feeling	100
Crows in Winter	101
Under the Pine	102
House for Sale	103
Poems after Paul Celan	
Corona	104
Flower	105
In Praise of Distance	106
Menhir	107
With Changing Key	108
Ich bin allein	109
The Whitest Dove of All	110
Sleep Then	111
Sleep and Food	112
I Heard It Said	113

From
THE OTHER MEANING

BEDLAM HILLS

Corroded flat as hills allow,
stubbled with stones and brittle weeds,
only the thorn blooms here
and scatters its seeds.

The hills are blank and pale now
beneath the clear and static air.
The landscape is as empty
as a blindman's stare.

Mad Clare, the story tells,
gathered her sticks and pieces here.
Her mind wore on the open rock.
But we forget Clare,

walk over and over the hills of strewn
and fractured rock where the berry
suckles the given stone
and the light breaks clearly.

These are the cold, the worn hills
with madness in their monotone
and emptiness where no life moves
beneath a stone.

BIRD SANCTUARY

I came down to the tideless bay
from hills sketched in rain
to light that flickers the pencil reed
to where these swans remain

and sail with slim and supple necks
over the water's rippled weed,
with necks and shadows seeking
in the cautious lengthened shade:

not knowing I would find
these water birds moving
in an area of meaning,
wings folded from flight —

or that swans on water glance
and settle into meaning
as thoughts and poems
on the edge of silence.

And there, now here these seven swans,
this water-world's remembered skies
hold silence, weed and living shade
within my centre of surprise.

OLD MEN ARE FACTS
The Ship's Graveyard, Risdon

When I was a boy I heard the sea upstairs in a shell.
I wanted to climb the spiral of sound
and make my life in its white storm:
its great storms were a part of me —
O part of me I have not found.

I spun the globe beneath my hand
and every port was a hive of love:
the fever hid along her mouth:
but I was young with a storm in my head
and over the north lay my cold south.

There is a life in facts: old men are facts:
I am a fact we all live through.
My face is old like the back of a shell
and I say less than I can tell.

Old men are facts as cabins are that bend the grass,
as funnels are like empty trees.
And yes these ships were washed up here
by fallen seas
to die along the withering shore;
I am an old man in a narrow hut;
these ships are part of me like memories;
and yes these portholes stare out my lame years
and in the dark and closing night
I turn life over in my hand.

Even if I could tell you of that land,
that subtle country of my heart,
I would only say in the windy shade:
old men are part of what they make and what is made.

FISHERMEN, WINTER

In the bay across the broken threshold sand
beyond the turning of the bird-walked beach,
deserted as a room — though birds and jetsam and
flotsam are always there — each belonging to each:

all morning they have sat there silent and alone
in a dinghy rocking on the sea like a gull,
while the mad beach birds for hours flown
and knocked by the light that cuts like a stone

walk on the wheeling water, tread the broken glass of
   the air . . .
And light congeals on faces, a wing or a hand . . .
In the tides of shadows the slow nets drag
where the bells of the sea ring into the land.

From the land: the dinghy rocking gently as a gull,
they work and drag their nets as patient as the sea,
who gather what it offers: fish, crab and shell;
letting slip the shadows, the light of wings, the sea.

WINTER FORESHORE

The drilling wind, the whittling air
these cruel tortured days
could eat the feeling in the mind
to the thought beneath despair:
we are our elegies of praise;

our going through is all.
These objects caught in light,
discarded anchor, sodden bird,
the wind-rhyming shell
reveal the heart is desolate.

Worm-wood hull and ruined shore,
the sharp thrust of splintered wood
scratch the mind with shapes of pain;
severed now, this one bird's claw
rejects the traitor tide.

Under the ravaging brittle wind
anchor, stone and driftwood lie:
dragged in a net of sentiment
they'll clutter up the mind —
till they become an elegy

or riveted to praise
endure the traffic of the heart.
Our winter shore is leashed to a tide
that covers all. But we must build:
build from the havoc of our days.

ALOES AND SEA

The aloes stand along the shore
and stitch the driftwood of the sea
to a nest of air and broken shells —
a honeycomb of air and bubbles.

The paddock shifts into the sea,
the lip of earth hangs on the air:
the aloe blades flash in the sun
but the stringy roots cry, "Where

is the stone to bind us fast,
to grip and hold us firm
against the wind, the tearing sea,
the night and subtle storm

that gnaws the earth along its nerve
and only leaves its caves of air?"
The aloes stand along the shore
and stitch the driftwood to the tides

and grope for the fallen binding stone
and cry, "Why is this storm, why harm?"
But sea and wind along the shore
seem to moan, "Reclaim, reclaim."

PENGUIN
near Fluted Cape

You strut above the littered shore
with scissors for a voice,
that cut against the stubborn wind
like ice against ice;
and nest within the north sunlight
and build within your season's tide,
and reconcile the sea and land —

you walk with fragile pride
between the edge of the jetsam sea
and the changing ledge of rock and tree
where you defy the storm and calm,
whose storm and calm move with each other
and knit like bones within your shape
the ice of the scoured south
and the north-black of the cape.

FISHERMEN, DROWNED BEYOND THE WEST COAST
to Chris Koch

Someone said dead men make islands in the sea
but there are no trees, no green islands
growing from these mouths and hollow eyes.
Under the areas of empty sea they lie,
fishermen drowned in a storm all miles from land.
There are no trees growing from their broken eyes,
no island gathered round their love and pain,
only a sudden emptiness, a sea of noise and silence
that hurts the ear's dead drum.

Wind and sea grow over and under the open storm,
the quick and pointless tyranny of nets that tied their
    hands,
and fish caged forever in the boat's square well;
drowned in their fumbling nets all miles from land
and their boat storm-rolled like a dead bird in the sea.

But I think they are separated now; the nets unravelled;
the heavy wood floats anywhere, water-logged and split,
alone in all the areas of sea. Only
the nets and fish and storm kept them together
as men — and they were not lonely.

There are no green islands for the coastless birds;
no trees branching from those eyes to hang a thought
    upon;
nothing, nothing that the hands can find:
only another island, quiet and simple, forming in
    another mind.

MAN WITH GREYHOUNDS

A man walks greyhounds on the morning frost.
They breathe and whine in the streetlight air
past the tired gates and scratch-dry lawns
to a city beach with a row of gums,
and all his dreams are running there
like the whirling dogs and the electric hare.

The man walks the street at six on the frost,
his smooth dogs strain the leather leash.
I hear them pant on the milkbottle air,
their muscles tight in a muzzle's cage.
The man in his cardigan goes and is lost
where his dreams race on the beach of his wish.

He walks for dreams where his dogs all win
on the track coming first a mile ahead.
I have heard the greyhounds tear at the leash
and howl on the frost where the dead beach goes.
I have heard him walk the dogs of his wish
tight in a muzzle with a leash a leash.
We are men with dreams in the frost
whose dreams become what we are most.

THIS TIME OF CALM

Who walks by the sea, this time of calm,
learns its meaning or the heart's:
tide's lull unwinds the intricate storm;
the swerving bird glides out of harm,
finding this sheltered hour home.

Who walks the wall or the shore's edge,
sees more than this wreckage of a storm:
kelp or the delicate spine of a fish,
more than a scoured branch, a long shell,
or the lap of water on a broken ledge:
sees the shell go under the sand
and the sand go under the sea;

sees all peril, all world's harm
contains this time of living calm;
sees walls battered and destroyed,
the intricate storm ensnare the calm;
learns its meaning is the heart's.
The sea inherits from itself always
and even in travelled seas new islands form.

IN SUMMER RAIN

While summer rain makes green the air
my easy birds sing through their fear
and point on straws of stubbled light
over their paddocks of delight.

Where in the rain the leaning hill
unwinds in flats of yellow, all
these orchards in my summer
defy the winters I remember.

And there's no need to tell me why
the world's the world or I am I:
when summer rain makes green the air
my easy birds shake off their fear

in rounded drops of simple rain;
they sing beyond the world of pain,
transcend the country of despair
and dance and point on calms of air.

Over the orchards' gentle light
in circles warm with warm delight
they sing the simple joy of rain.
O may this joy in joy remain.

DESERTED BANDSTAND, KINGSTON BEACH

Turning from the sketched pines
and the tedious esplanade
I always find this frame,

this loud rotunda's dancing red:
a bandstand empty twenty years;
an object deserted —

but not those brazen afternoons
a girl and a fumbling boy
discovered the wandering dunes.

Gone the band, the uniform;
stays the silent rusting frame.
Gone the kiss — and yet

only the moment's different.
They heard the sharp and dazzled
cry of a gull

above their Sunday band,
the flat and curious light.
She led his seeking hand.

And they are all here:
the sea in a shell,
an echo's silence in the mind:

each making the other real.
This round and failing red,
the promised girl and her lover ...

No image can ever be deserted.

PORTUGUESE LAUREL, FLOWERING

Distance can put beauty on
and nearness take it off:
this laurel tree alive with light
reconciles both.

It stands a harp of loosened fire
strung to praise the world
and gathers distance in itself:
the foiled shaken cloud,

spray and foam and floating snow,
burning buds of stars,
the Milky Way and the trailing light
of long light years.

Its nearness makes its splendour ours.
Those branches laced with light
are rooted in our tragic world:
confusion breaks through in delight.

As petals on a bough
our frail world hangs there.
Rocked in summer's violent gale
torn and built from the air

this lyre of lightning, stars and snow
and working petals holds
our distance and our nearness in
and celebrates both worlds.

THE LAST SUMMER

The hawk with heavy-lidded eyes
falls through a world of loaded skies,
falls and tears the light with its eye:
falling hawk and falling sky.

Falling, falls, falling dies:
the hawk with drought inside its eyes;
fruit falls and splits and dries,
falls with fullness, falls with weight,
the hawk falls alive with hate.
Weight of colour, weight of years:
how can fruit contain its years,
the hawk its tense and nervous hate?
Black and red and blue and gold
falling, fall, cannot withhold.

And like a knife a scarlet bird
sings deserts in the lemon trees.

The light is torn across with black,
the mountain sings alive with hate;
red and gold and green and black
cathedral trees fall through the air
and burn the earth to love and hate.
O trees burn and purge despair
and crash like churches through the air

while like a knife a scarlet bird
sings deserts in the lemon trees.

LATE AUTUMN DOVE

O see where settling now and taking shape
within this park the light defines,
in the frames of trees and scribbled leaves
winter is sketched in a death of lines:

a fret of wings disturbs the air,
wings dazzling in a fan of light
as a dove tumbles, gently falls
down the space of its brilliant flight.

And see: a trembling dove defies
scrabbled winter's taut despair:
lives into joy, accepts the last light
falling, falling through the air.

EQUINOX

Hills, the slow anxiety of change,
open in the green of farms;
sheep or clouds the sheltered day
shows girls like trees with flowers in their arms

and miles of orchards, caught in spring,
weave nets of light across the air,
but a blue moth's bewildered wing
defines the season in its snare

where down by the fern-dark creek
winter's orchid dies again
and tense in the orchard's nervous warmth
a rooster treads a scarlet hen.

PRAYING MANTIS

O yogi, mantis, preying leaf
and subtle balance of this green,
within your eye the rolling world
is centred where the nervous fly
drinks the dew's one point of light —
O double meaning of your prayer.

And you, equation of the green,
as tense as thought, can link a world
where you are leaf and leaf is you
until you've trapped the careless fly
within the logic of your spell —
And then and only then can leaves
distinguish what this green can't tell.

THE OTHER MEANING

There is another meaning here — in birds
and trees, in love and grief,
in the fall of the blown leaf
and pain and joy shuffled and dealt like cards
— where thoughts in my stubborn land of pain
travel like water over stone.

But I have failed again: failed love
and failed those simple trees that hold
their brief and formal birds, the standing shade;
my steeple world bereaves its bells.

Even now with winter's first red bird,
the hard incisive light and snow beginning
I have failed: finding the world alive
with pain, and without its other meaning.

ALCESTE
to Gwen Harwood

"My need too for beginnings drove me here
to a mountain charred by the moon and sun
where a hawk drowning in a lake of air
tears the light with claws of pain.
And here upon the mountain in the snow
I find myself alone and still accursed.
A beginning is a need, a way to go.
There is no image for the spirit's thirst.

I sought this last extremity of mind:
my need for order killed the heart
and brought me to this place alone
with nothing but dry cliffs of stone
and a tall house in a waste of ice.

I came out here for solace, a recluse
against the nightmare of the world,
where hawk and stone seemed reconciled.

But what can grow in slate and stone?
Though meanings grow in the defiled
chaotic cities of the brain,
the sterile is the simply reconciled.

And now I know that I must turn and go
to the seething cities of the plain,
that here my meanings cannot grow
in the dumb splendour of the sterile snow

that even there the light is thorned with pain."

THE SHADOW

Something in the landscape
attentive, stares at me:
nothing's shape or shape of fear
it watches discreetly.

And I would fly away
far from its captive gaze
that tries to trap my wings
safe in its silent ways —

or being toad could hide
alone in the bubbling mud
and lost in secret darkness
grow jewels in my head;

or being fish could swim
away from its tender hand
that tries to coax me slyly
back to the stable sand.

And yet I can't avoid
its careful prying ways;
its tiny thread of pain
links my different days —

or the way in a sudden street
it mocks and distorts me.
But when I am falling
it holds and supports me.

THYLACINE

They'll not find him in the hills
above the slow fern gully;
he's gone to earth like a sunken creek
in an unknown valley;

nor find the fur on the bent thorn
nor hear him moan at the raw moon:
he stalks down the valley of the years
with his old love, his old pain.

They'll not find him in the hills:
he's gone to earth in an unknown valley
with legends of coal and Time in stone,
with the sly fern, with the gully.

THESE WRENS, THIS WATTLE TREE

These wrens, this wattle tree,
the rapid blue, the sheltered green
on the sandy bracken hill
dance their colour in my mind,
swerve a meaning to the heart:
nor any meaning heart can find.

Above the wastes of yellow thorn
and dry moss stones, in steady shade,
they flash their blue within this green,
O into shadow, out of shade
they swerve their colour through the air
and dance a meaning for the mind:
be where the song is, heart be there.

MYTH

The child ran to find the bird,
light and fire, water, air,
weeds and shells and sullen fish,
the bird that grew inside her wish,
singing "Here O here, come here."

The garden opened like a room;
she ran through halls of flowers, wings;
the fountain splashed the weed, the fish.
"Here O here; it's here it sings."

And see the pond fulfils a sky,
the water opens like a door,
a water snail has no horn.
The light is black and slightly torn.
O hear the bird: it sings once more.

And then the water shut on her
and raped her mind, while fish and weeds
struggled in her party frock.
Her bangle broke its coloured beads.

Above the trees sang loud with birds:
the light was bruised, the garden torn:
below the fish swam on and on.
She floated on the water, born
into a fierce and dying swan.

From
AN ISLAND SOUTH

AT AN EXHIBITION OF HISTORICAL PAINTINGS, HOBART

The sadness in the human visage stares
out of these frames, out of these distant eyes;
the static bodies painted without love
that only lack of talent could disguise.

Those bland receding hills are too remote
where the quaint natives squat with awkward calm.
One carries a kangaroo like a worn toy,
his axe alert with emphasised alarm.

Those nearer woollen hills are now all streets;
even the water in the harbour's changed.
Much is alike and yet a slight precise
disparity seems intended and arranged —

as in that late pink terrace's façade.
How neat the houses look. How clean each brick.
One cannot say they look much older now,
but somehow more themselves, less accurate.

And see the pride in this expansive view:
churches, houses, farms, a prison tower;
a grand gesture like wide-open arms
showing the artist's trust, his clumsy power.

And this much later vision, grander still:
the main street sedate carriages unroll
towards the tentative, uncertain mountain:
a flow of lines the artist can't control —

the foreground nearly breaks out of its frame
the streets end so abruptly in the water . . .
But how some themes return. A whaling ship.
The last natives. Here that silent slaughter

is really not prefigured or avoided.
One merely sees a profile, a full face,
a body sitting stiffly in a chair:
the soon-forgotten absence of a race . . .

Album pieces: bowls of brown glazed fruit . . .
I'm drawn back yet again to those few studies
of native women whose long floral dresses
made them first aware of their own bodies.

History has made artists of all these
painters who lack energy and feature.
But how some gazes cling. Around the hall
the pathos of the past, the human creature.

WINTER

Winter in this city's world:
and city parks inform my days
with distance, silence, and a song of birds.
Winter is the heart of praise.

In praise of clarity the winds blow
from the cold south across the hills
and shake the pear tree free of snow —
and slam the door
upon unmade decisions in a room.

Winter's ways are not our ways.
O slow and secret corridor
into an inward clarity of days;
O winter at the heart of praise.

DESPITE THE ROOM

Into this cave of night, darkness
and the sleepless, tired room,
despite my mind, the heavy blind,
the sudden song of birds will come

to draw me out into the light,
to walk the path and feel the day
surround me with its cool and green,
dew saying all it has to say

in drops that glance along the leaf
or in the rose, asleep unfurled:
the patient strictness of the dew,
the slow intactness of the world.

REFLECTIONS

Is this the self I thought I knew within
this narrow world of helpless self-concern,
where in fatigue huge images begin
to grope at knowledge, thinking to discern

recognitions, motives slyly caught,
suspicions looming in a hostile sky.
Hell is other people, Sartre thought.
The threat of others, ill-will, all my I . . .

And knowing in myself this edge of spite,
afraid of chaos, and of order, too,
a sense of balance which is rarely right,
I think of one now whom I hardly knew

who dreamt of constant threats against her life,
slights to a vast, imagined reputation;
saw in each glance intentions of a knife
to slash at her with pointless imputation.

The ego has such dramas of its own
and sudden lapses back into the sheer
world of acceptance that it thought outgrown,
but needs its sickness as a dog needs fear

and fleas, to know a certain sense of life.
Her mirror-world delusions are my own.
To break the long reflections of her strife
she filled each pocket with a clean white stone

and drowned herself face downwards in a stream
so shallow that it hardly wet her hair.
I wonder if the nightmare turned to dream
and how far down descended her despair.

I only know one tendency is mine:
to walk with images that change and chill
the contours of reality's design
along the failing tightrope of the will.

RETURN OF THE PRODIGAL SON

Years of terror, in the mud of years,
absent from the self; the self alone;
wounded like an animal and nothing real
but the closed reality of pain

as hard and shut as stone, the thorn, the land —
not even knowing that he took a way;
but only that a change can bring relief —
not even seeing, even knowing what to say

to those who passed him on the furtive road,
or any thought to see his father stand
beneath a palm tree in a fly-blown shade;
unaware of body, face, or hand:

he stumbled on the roadway in the sun,
a mirage or a vision, falling, fell
and broke into the country of his heart
and lay there drinking by its dying well.

O life that beat his head against the road,
O seed, oasis, O consenting heart.
Black with light a fountain wept.
And knowing nothing, knew he must depart.

FOR MY DAUGHTER

Made from nothing: bud and rose,
kisses, water, mystery:
you who grew inside our need
run, in your discovery,

out of the garden's folded light,
out of the green, the fountain's spray,
past the shrubs, the dew-lit ferns,
out to the noise, the street, the day:

and stand, in your astonishment,
beneath the hanging heavy limes
(O my child, O my darling daughter,
summer was full of wars and crimes)

to see the foal, the clown, the doll,
the circus and procession band
march up the street and march away ...
And so you turn and take my hand.

ABSENCE

This afternoon by the fuchsia tree
the garden sang with heat and shade;
the sails of yachts moved idly down
the lapsing green unsheltered river,
and in the park two children played;
shells, a necklace, carelessness.
The tree above me like your dress
sang of the warmth its silence made.

Tonight at home: the moth-wings of the air.
We live our lives in solitary rooms.
The gardens slope towards the sea
the ferry plies and frail gardens
bend the water, falls the park.
I touch your absence everywhere.
My words go feeling for you in the dark.

SUMMER BAND CONCERT

Tired with its dogs and doves
the park's distracted tunes
sprawl across the littered green,
these slow and tedious afternoons.

And there a brassy serenade
and here two lovers come to rest.
Beneath a pampered laurel tree
he leans his head against her breast.

And round and round the waltzes go:
smeared lollies in a bag;
the formal tunes and gardens merge:
the light exhausts, the music drags —

and sleep condemns the lovers' eyes
the gardens blind ... He draws her near
and puts his arm beneath her back
and whispers darkness in her ear.

EARLY ARRIVAL: SYDNEY

Red cockatoo crests caught on coral-trees:
my Sydney emblems. Dragging the land in view
our ship hauls glass and concrete to its side
as gulls fly up and snatch and scream and glide
away on a sea smeared with a trace of blue.

The neons flicker and the skyline wakes.
The orange suburbs float through miles of calm;
a pastel-coloured terrace shades its slope.
While five gulls fight for nothing on a rope,
the breeze picks out a single listless palm.

The city's like a room far under sea
with locked arcades where shadow-waves subside.
Grey windows bend great cloud-shapes as they pass.
Beyond these tiles, tunnels, iron, glass,
the flat waters of green inlets ride
where all the folded yachts are chained away.

But here the huge hotels still sway in space
with the exactness of a foreign place.

SUMMER SKETCHES: SYDNEY

i
City of yachts and underwater green
with blue hydrangeas fading in between
the walls of sloping gardens full of sails,
as sudden as a heart the sunlight fails
and over all the city falls again
a change of light, the neon's coloured rain.

ii
Tourists in their lives of sudden ease
stare through dark glasses at the coral-trees
and know at once that only colour's true:
the red in green: within the green, the blue.

iii
At night the cool precision of the stars,
the neon glitter and the sexy cars,
the easy pick-up in the close green bars.

iv
A holiday like some smooth magazine;
how photos can improve the simplest scene.
They isolate the image that endures;
beyond the margins is the life that cures.
But when the surface gloss is thought away
some images survive through common day
and linger with a touch of tenderness:
the way you brushed your hair, your summer dress.

RETURN TO HOBART

We leave behind the farms, the aerodrome,
the tall unfinished bridge. Near the centre
a rent-an-Avis-car sign says we're home;
the airways' office empty as we enter.

Stunned in their Sunday lunar vacancy
the streets assert that life needs style, façades.
Shop windows like aquariums of clouds;
and round about the hills, the dry backyards.

A gull stands on one leg in Fitzroy Place.
Salvation Army Band with precise labour
plays hymns that wrench me back to ten years old:
the war years and Yank ships in the harbour,

and still late yachts slice through the summer breeze.
My taxi swerves into a dug-up street
with half a road unfinished. Home again.
Challenged by change, the sense of the incomplete.

PHILOCTETES
In a private hotel

Never a thought of coming or of going:
rotting in his tenement of pain,
he cries aloud and walks his room again.
Outside it's winter and the sky and snowing.

Take him, stick, arthritic and alone,
and feel his way down twenty rented stairs;
avoid the hallway mirror of his fears;
the fig leaf on the statue covers stone;

and walk him through his world of vacant pain:
and take him, take him where he's going —
to buy the evening paper — always knowing
when to turn and walk him back again.

FAMILY ALBUM

i
Playing with a tomahawk, a gun,
the children in the weeded formal garden
pitch their Christmas tents and just for fun
whet their axes and the blades they harden

chop off screams and squeals within the dusk
that splays each other's hair with pats of mud.
Upstairs the adolescent and athletic son
glimpses heaven from his tower of blood

and riding like his hero's motorbike
crashes into nowhere-all-is-well.
Mother calls the youngsters in to tea.
The light filters. Somewhere rings a bell.

ii
A bell rings. And father shuts his book.
A constipated blowfly sings the praise
of summer in its iridescent wings . . .
Father notes the young ones' little ways

and how they've torn his prize azalea out;
is wise; remembers how he too was young;
and watering the roses he recalls
the tender taste of his wife's tongue —

and how he praised her body with his own
and made her flower like a burning tree;
and standing in the garden's fading green
dreams of a little sad adultery.

QUIET EVENING

i
The inner weather's not the outer scene:
they sail dinghies through the flooded slums
and dozers clear a road that caused a car
to crash and hurtle through the planted gums.

A smell of petrol weighs the street,
insists, oppresses. And the neon glare
provokes a headache's pulse of pain . . .
The statues with their tarnished stare

ignore the damaged park, the flooded drain,
the twisted vista and the *Toast and Tea* . . .
Arrives my suburb bus that flounders home
like a green porpoise through a daggered sea.

ii
Blooms my tropical flower of gas . . .
The shapes of simple and coherent life
surround me and define me from without;
that moment pierces like a sudden knife.

But later take a bath and then a book;
someone bashes someone down below;
a furtive slips his key in Madam Y's;
I hear him enter. And for all I know

someone enters Cyril's round the back.
The moment loosens and the doorways glide
Pandora's monsters: O my dear I'm too
broadminded to be horrified.

And reading how I dream I might have been
a golden youth with narrow hips and thighs
adored on beaches by wet girls and queens,
Pandora's monsters or her butterflies:

I'm too controlled. I make them fly away.
It floods outside as if disaster's near.
I light a cigarette. I'm glad my mind's
so elegant, so various and clear.

DEATHBED SKETCH
for an unnamed portrait, signed

At last a page is turning. Change of scene.
That once young poet's power's failing fast
and I must jot down quickly what occurred
before his name's a footnote in the past.

His first book made him known to a small band;
it passed in the antipodes for Art,
with verses full of God and sex and wars.
It proved he had no ear and far less heart.

And yet it was encouraged as things go:
the sturdy thinness of our cultural scene
makes anything half literate appear
a contribution to the might-have-been

which still defines our future and our past.
But let's attack the few who really matter —
those without talent, art's sly parasites,
these we caress, cajole, and slowly flatter.

The early ideal, the true poet's vision,
the search to find a language and a voice
was hardly his to lapse from or regret;
a certain cunning had defined his choice.

Art itself, Art as he understood it,
Art was a way to conquer and impress;
he'd long known that his favourite type of woman
enjoyed an artist's hand beneath her dress ...

And men too showed an interest in his skills.
One said,"I just love everything he writes",
but later he confessed he most preferred
the fluent figure in its swimming tights.

In time our poet found his public role;
opinion-making offers sure returns
as those who trade in reputations find —
theirs is the first the careless goddess spurns.

Appeared as poet-critic on TV:
"Poets are good at stirring others up."
Increasing dangers of complacency
followed by *Comments on the Melbourne Cup*.

He stood amazed to see his small part growing,
an invitation here, addresses there;
"When all I want to be is with the Muse
my social conscience leads me to despair" —

It was a way to keep conviction flowing,
though like the most successful he'd soon learned
contempt for others and their slow goodwill:
a certain arrogance is never spurned.

He always found the crowd that needed him
to tell them what to think, to set their fashion
in Art and comment: "The whole country needs
my kind of person's tragic sense of mission."

He kept his name in print with book reviews,
his verse appeared in his own magazine:
"It gives a wider vista to my views.
Here in a land where Judith Wright is queen

of lady poets and poor Alec Hope
has let the team down badly with his verse,
I must turn critic, speak aloud the truth.
Without my voice things would be even worse."

He chose publicity. He chose display.
Rage for success at all costs drove him on;
but like a dancer who's outlived his prime,
knew he could now be neither prince nor swan

nor merely someone watching from the wings.
"I can't keep up as every writer must . . .
Torn between TV and my Lit Fund Lectures,
why poetry — it's just — a sort of lust."

"I'll never write again," he used to smile,
"this country's done my talent too much harm";

and saw within the mirror how the leaks
were slowly spreading through his schoolboy charm.

And yet from time to time a verse appeared
saying how big men are compared with birds;
and these were one day gathered in a second
book that was merely ideas set to words.

Of course we all agreed we would be kind,
haunted by our own sense of deeper failure.
It's human not to keep your standards high.
We need his type of person in Australia.

BUS RIDE

Coming home tonight
in the green electric bus,
I brush past strapless girls
hearing old people fuss,

and stand here in my jeans,
always troubled by sex,
watching the way hair curls
on a choice of a dozen necks

and press as close as I can
to two or three bright bits
tight in their coloured skirts,
and stare and stare at their tits ...

If I could get my hands
on a warm split of a peach,
touch alone would show
we have no need of speech;

as if she were a lake
I'd swim and slowly dive
and drive her into shore,
giving her dead-alive.

I dream of bowls of fruit,
say pawpaws in a dish.
The smell of love is ah
carnations, water, fish.

I'd do you anywhere,
in cars or dunes, near trees.
You'd find, cool budding girl,
I give uncommon ease;

and when I lie with you
and know your tree in flower,
this fiercest tenderness
grows from the sweetest power:

a violence of light,
a summer storm in the dark;
voice of the crouching lion,
the blind force of the lark.

And staring at your face
and through your summer dress,
the dry mouth of lust
flows with tenderness.

WRONG TURNING

Relapses and wrong turnings find the way
to the still garden where with dew the rose
hangs upside down in water, and the light's
at rest in the bud it chose.

Always it's at hand: the promised tree,
the pool of silence and the dreaming swan
that moves in its world of waiting and consent ...
Always these remain, though we are gone

relapsing and wrong-turning and confused;
impatience, desperation; all resist ...
Lost now in your maze say, I have failed.
But the swan and the garden and the rose exist.

ONE SEASON

This is one season of the heart's dismay
when life is like a strident conversation;
words pretend there's something left to say
when silence simply covers consternation.

Discordant season: moments of despair:
we glimpse the cracks that run all through our lives;
the heart we lightly thought rich and austere;
the mind's disordered drawer of borrowed knives.

Don't run with words. Don't seek them. Words aren't wise.
The mind's eclipses move to prove its suns.
And nudity of all is best disguise:
stay bare in stillness ... Vanity runs.

AN EFFECT OF LIGHT

Swans in their grey and silver park
hiss from the reeds their indignation
where looking back to what was wake
the pool suggests a moment's agitation ...

After work in solitary rooms
I've sought this hour in the tranquil park
where things assume their proper shapes again,
as trees and steeples for the waiting dark.

Work I say. It's self-work that I mean.
Days and hours full of disarray
when life is a discarded scratched-out note
one cannot read ... And how can words convey

this sense without an image for the mind?
Life's promised tapestry grows more undone;
or does one merely see the underside,
where to observers burns a modest sun?

I would ask this as clearly if I could
as that white dove that's tumbling in the sky:
how can a sense of meaning still persist
so intertwined with sense of no reply?

I turn towards the sight of paddling swans.
What is confusion but no attitude;
or is tranquillity a touch of light
that merely lingers till the mind's subdued?

I watch the fussing wings across the pool
and wonder what it means, regeneration;
and see within the circles ruffling out,
the waterlily's simple revelation.

DIALOGUE

And so you see your life before you
not like mountains seen through trees,
but like a book of shapeless poems:
glittering felicities

but botched and not a verse that works,
the brilliant image and the random phrase,
but where's the poem? It's not here before you
in days divided into different ways.

And so you say perfection's not for man,
and that is true: but laziness you mean.
Division has its comforts like despair:
the odd convenience of the in-between.

But look, these words are wrong, a verbal play:
despair is voiceless or is not at all.
Distraction and evasion aren't implied
as man's whole nature since his primal fall.

Let's face the facts: this is a botched-up job;
these days, these verses don't belong to art.
You must begin again and turn and trust
the deep resistant silence of the heart.

THERE IS NO SLEIGHT OF HAND

There is no sleight of hand
not caught by art's reflection.
Poetry which can't pretend
is perfect lie-detection.

Who knows what echoes then
the song of chaos finds?
A self-intoxicated tune
dazzles, confounds, and blinds.

Dismay is all its load,
it has no way to take;
but words on their proper road
dance for the spirit's sake.

Let candour be your guide
and may your words rejoice
in art's only reward
to speak in one's own voice.

BEYOND THIS POINT

Driven here by dry and traceless need,
need to be silent, simply to be alone,
I half-observe a grey gull's sense of speed —
shaft of feathers, wing of delicate bone —
and how late shadows break the slope of land,
making the dunes recede and then resist.
A worn rock drags the light down through the sand,
casting a shadow finer than a wrist.

Beyond this point there's only waste and sea;
a vast absence; wind like a waterfall.
The inhuman has such perfect clarity:
pebble and bone, light on the old seawall:
lucidity that leaves life scoured out.
Light at its brightest turns to dark and dazes.
Pebble and bone and triton shell's blunt snout.
It's the abundant, varied, that amazes.

FOR A NEW YEAR

The new year came with rain and sudden thunder,
a late walk on this thin suburban beach,
watching drab doves picking on the shore;
with modest comic steps they flutter under
the Moreton Bays where my gaze cannot reach.
One slowly hovers, then is lost once more.

And turning from my past, my sunken year,
I drag old resolutions into view,
astonished by the shapelessness of things.
Ahead lie oceans, mountains, ports of fear,
those problems that no facing can subdue;
but may the year bring too the certainty that sings.

Whatever sustains us, nature, powers above,
we live by risk and change and sheer surprise:
the fold of a wing, a sudden precision of blue.
Despair transfixes what it cannot move,
but expectation changes hands and eyes.
Love is the totally unexpected view

and being, need prove nothing to the world.
The fanatic's fiercest need is to avoid
the doubts his certainty distils as hate.
Convictions are not bombs that must be hurled,
but what remain, intact and undestroyed,
though changed by the things we can't eliminate

as light is changed by intervening leaves.
We neither live by dogma nor by theory:
still even without orders there's relation.
I cannot grasp the whole my heart believes.
But watch that sparrow hunt that butterfly:
life's nonsense pierces too with strange elation

and through what's most absurd my heart is riven
and out of sight both bird and butterfly . . .
and still and still my sense of joy persists.
What we cannot grasp can still be given;
and intertwined with every rooted why
such tenderness, such joy exists.

LATE APRIL: HOBART

Turning from the mirror full of leaves
that draws the autumn garden through the room
I note that brown's the colour of decay,
but in the garden how it just achieves
a sense of balance between rot and bloom
where old chrysanthemums lean all one way

as if an angle meant avoiding change.
Thick with its burden of excess and loss
this time of year depresses and elates:
all points of stillness hover out of range;
wind strips the season to its sticks and dross
and days to a blue scratched out of southern slates.

This autumn garden is decay of gold,
a waste of mildew, fading reds that glow
as in bare boughs the brown and gold respond.
Each day the corners lengthen shades of cold
and silver rain gives way to mountain snow
and black and sour grows the lily pond.

Gone are the statements of the summer dawn
when love grew more abundant with excess;
sustained by filth, fertility survives.
Fulfilment needs its time to be withdrawn
in its own silence, much like holiness.
In time each shifting harmony arrives.

And now it's this dark brevity of gold
with so much withering as colours glow
as if the frugal with the fecund mates.
The sunlight dazzles with its April cold
and through the red the brown begins to show.
Beneath it all such final bareness waits.

WARMTH IN JULY: HOBART
Sybille's

Warmth in July like first clear days of spring,
and sunlight glints in mirrors, windows, pools;
the heat hangs in the garden like a stare.
The light is still abrupt with winter's sting
but change is upon us; change is everywhere.

The sun shows nothing but a strict repose:
a net of trees, each twig a wired nail;
I look as through a cage into the sky
and see beyond the blue this season chose
the strident blue within a peacock's tail.

Why should this warmth remind me of my death?
And could I bear such clarity while dying?
Such hard precision suggests nothing more.
The sharpness of the light has caught my breath
with so much stillness. Not one insect flying.

The light is caught: no shadow overflows.
And nothing's yet begun. No season's ended.
All buds are merely knowledge in the mind.
Implicit in the twig are hip and rose;
but waiting, waiting too is still intended.

We seek too soon the end, the final things;
we try to grasp the whole where meanings start
in detail that may never reach design.
But feel the light and how it soaks and stings
and taste the blue where branches fall apart

till all your knowledge is mere warmth and glow,
all apprehension — as of sensual ease:
a sense of sure precision deep in things.
The year has still its separate months to go
but change is promised and awakenings.

From
FAMILIAR PLACES

VIEW FROM THE DOMAIN, HOBART

Small town, dull town; nothing further south;
jagged cape, smooth hills, the neat flat river valley,
the harbour with an island in its mouth.
Whichever way I look a road extends
along a hilltop or a thin cleared gully.

A city you can block out with your hands
from vantage points like this inside your car —
though something of the uncontained persists.
Those three odd farms, those shacks beyond the sands,
the outhouse on the hill are just too far
to fit into the pattern of your fists.

The off shape of backyards, the flat brick walls,
and every inner hill contains a steeple.
Across a sportsfield one last runner crawls.
My old school stands in fading pink cement,
and men on yellow dozers clear a road
through the half suburbs where my childhood went.

Could other places now mean other styles?
I catch the way the bridge divides the harbour
and wonder what it is my future fears:
the small anonymous life of love and labour,
or growing coarse and cautious with the years?

BALMORAL SUMMER '66

All day the weight of summer and the shrill
spaced flight of jet planes climbing north.
The news at half past twelve brought further crimes.
Insane dictators threaten new disasters.

The light of summer with its bone-white glare
and pink hibiscus in the yacht club garden.
The beach is strewn with bodies of all sizes.
How the sight of human nudity surprises —
cleft buttock, shaved armpit, nipple hair.

The heat haze hovers over Grotto Point
and skiers skim the violent flat water.
Incredible the feats that art demands.

Submarines surface to refuel
around this headland in a small bay's stillness.
History encroaches like an illness.
And children chase the gulls across the sand.

SUMMER NOTES

Dead summer will not yield. Green stones
are all the garden has to show and they
will not solve all our problems of decay.
The wind heaves and the scraped palm moans.

In the fruit basket lemons turn to fur,
a beard grows where an orchid filled a pot.
Downstairs my sleeping daughter starts to stir.
Soon she'll outgrow her squeaking, creaking cot.

Growth and growth; the hair, the nails, the teeth.
How many sheep and cattle we consume
tearing at the flesh inside a room.
The mind alone cannot know such relief.

Rough surfaces and old beds full of stones.
Young trees clamouring for stake and twine.
A thick grub like a pizzle eats the vine.
The season presses on my ageing bones.

POSTCARD FROM THE SUBTROPICS

This time is not my season, nor my tone:
dry distant lightning, storms that never start,
time of the writer's block, the shapeless dream of art.

Calligraphic lightning flicks the pewter sky.
Standing in the garden, I watch the citrus bugs
mating rear to rear, sucking the lemon dry.

The beetle that I touch sprays acid from its arse.
Alerted like a bird it lifts a scarlet wing
and flops from branch to branch. Cicadas whirr.
The garden starts to steam. The heat begins to sting.

Summer in the tropics: fungus time,
fungus in the mouth and on the skin.
Time of dry lightning, lines that never start,
and an art demanding vacant discipline.

A ROOM IN MOSMAN

A room in Mosman: year's end with a storm.
The vine on the veranda starts to heave.
All day the wind has blown the house about.
Beyond belief the need still to believe.

The sentimental rhetoric of rain
batters the garden's rubbish of torn leaves.
Such violence to leave such vacancy.
After the rain the light like broken glass.

House at a dead end; time of crude effects.
Beneath transfigurations the inane
waits like a broken fence beneath a vine,
a horde of leaves, an overflowing drain.

And what to make of this, and where begin?
Must this too still be sung, this inert slush?

I think of Chardin in Mongolia
and Nolan at the South Pole with a brush.

LINES FOR ROSAMOND McCULLOCH

Simple observation was your line:
rough hills, trees whipped by hail,
dhows off the coast of Arabia,
pears like mandolins, a snail.

Full view or sketch, you always returned
to coastlines of the south, ridged volcanic stone,
icebergs of rock, needles, unknown phares,
lakes seen from the air, shells like a telephone.

People were your weakness. How you'd make a face!
Different pools rewarded working on:
the Derwent drained to a sheet of stained foil,
backwaters, clouds, the irascible swan.

Your landscapes knew no people. They were home
and liberation for the overburdened life,
winds beating through the central hills.
You used your pencil like a surgeon's knife

and gave the island back the images it gave —
tide country with a sea fence for a frame.
The last dry sketch *Small fish in small pool*,
and *Disappearing wreck off Cape Fame*.

I still see your workroom, the pear near the door
repeating the leadlight repeating the vine.
You left me an etching of Eaglehawk Hills
and said to me once, "I'm the last of my line."

A FEW WORDS FOR MAXI

Dear Maxi, it's already seven years
you left us in your bandages and plaster,
smiling your sudden smile, refusing tears,
declaring I'm not getting younger faster —
and thirty years or more since you came here.
Your family park became the bonsai trees
you watered with a dropper for the moss,
and you became a Sydney Viennese.

There was so much we never spoke about.
The past you knew. We tried to stick to Strauss,
reciting bits from Hofmannsthal
and nodding at mots from Kraus.

Last summer I had twice hallucinations:
in one I thought I saw you at the Cross
standing with some shadows in the shade.
It was your presence and my sense of loss.

And when I pass your B'nai B'rith flat
I see you still alone with your last creeper
coiling its weekly way along the wall,
growing away, your illness growing deeper.

This is the season that you always loved
seeing the semi-tropics fade and bloom:
the surface of the sea stained shrill with light,
reflections waving through your darkened room
as all the windows of a tower of flats
catch the sun's last rays and start to glow.

I see you watching from your balcony,
yachts and gardens streaming away below.

FOR EDITH HOLMES: TASMANIAN PAINTER

I heard your living voice again last night,
your voice that mixed so many styles and tones,
an interview recorded before death —
you who detested wirelesses and phones.

I knew the way your life sustained your art,
your patient toil to get things down in paint.
I heard how strength remained though you complained
at eighty that the bloom was growing faint.

You spoke of your few teachers, then your friends.
You never had a theory but you knew
you had to go to France to learn to see
Mount Direction in its smoked-glass blue

and rediscover Bally Park through chalk.
Epergne with black grapes revealed your style,
with geese in backyard like a Roman frieze,
and still unfinished, child who wouldn't smile.

I met you in the last phase of your art
when all your subjects felt your full control:
a line became a branch became a tree
and wilting flowers revived in your clear bowl.

"I've had small recognition but enough,"
you said: "I live for colour and this place.
See that lichen's shawl spread on a rock.
For me the mountain has a human face,
the hills an outline that is partly mine . . ."

Your curtain with a window shows a life
but what your epoch struggled for is found
in breakfast room with mountain, bread and knife.

FOR NAN CHAUNCY: 1900-1970

Dear Nan, I've seen you twice again this week
as always only in the best of places.
Children's Book Week comes around again.
You smile at us across the library hall.
I wonder what you now make of it all?

I often dream of Chauncy Vale in spring
your wattle hedges raked by the cold breeze,
the cliff side where the children found a cave
hidden under ferns and trailing vines,
and everywhere adopted animals:
the emu who provided all your cakes,
the peacocks stately, sensual, hindoo,
the black devils and the half-trained goats.
Along the creek your acres of thick bulbs.

"I am a woman of two worlds you know
my generation still called England home;
that's something you won't ever have to do . . .
You must see Copenhagen once in June . . .
I love the word professional you know
I want to be a writer to the core".

"Come again" you'd say each time we left
with boxes full of flowers, eggs, bamboo:
giving was your only kind of speech.
"I must get back, my books are calling now.
They keep me living and the pennies rolling in.
I've got a new one coming on to boil.
You can't fob children off with whimsy now."

Last time there was no other time again.
You gave us feathers and some weathered glass:
"Come again before the year turns cold . . ."
You smile at us from the far library wall,
benign and level-headed, looking straight ahead
as if you saw the meaning of it all.
My daughters ask did she write all those books?
Looking for your secrets in your non-committal looks.

COINS AND BRICKS

Last night I found this box of darkened coins
and foxed notes printed in '44 —
an army minted millions for defeat.
They have no current value to restore
yet they meant fortune, life in that lost state.
Their only interest now is out of date.

This house was market style twelve years ago,
now it belongs with Tudor, Spanish Mission.
Boom Style, Colonial are back with Art Nouveau,
and Italianate is once more in the fashion.

And these brief stanzas neat as coins and bricks
depend upon the order they define.
Another time means other shapes and styles,
but what they hold for this small space is mine.

SLOPE WITH BOULDERS

Crouching down from the snow
refusing to turn around
aping sudden stillness,
they heave up from the ground

like sunken monuments,
torsos and bent shoulders
stained and patched in the rain,
statues turning to boulders.

All these million years
folding their arms and heads,
kneeling with backs to the road,
they watch for river beds.

Down from the slopes of ice,
wearing their lichen shrouds,
they feel near the creek's edge
the sway of mist and clouds.

Abandoned in the grass,
sketches that can't emerge,
like old ruined gods
their avenues converge.

They scatter like a team
baffled by rain and snow,
unable to make an end,
unable to let it go.

BACK IN HOBART

My point of reference is this summer slope,
these paddocks stacked like long plates of bread;
and at day's end, the black loaves of the hills.

I'm back in Hobart after years away
visiting remembered, holy places:
grey boulders in a small suburban creek,
the leopard-spotted plane-trees in the square.
The permanence of place does not recede:
the spiritual sky, the unencumbered air.

A cloudless day. Each carted stone in place.
My mother's house lapses in front of tended trees,
and to the left the mountain changes face . . .

Years ago in Paris I saw a threadbare robe
worn by a priest in 580 AD;
locked behind glass its tarnished red and gold.

Standing by the gate I recall the whole scene now
knowing how things change, and how they hold.

TWENTY YEARS OF SYDNEY

It's twenty years of Sydney to the month
I came here first out of my fog-bound south
to frangipanni trees in old backyards,
and late at night the moon distorting palms.

Even then the Cross was crumby, out of touch.
I was too timid for Bohemia as a style
or living long in rooms in dark Rose Bay hotels.
All one night a storm flogged herds of Moreton Bays,
for days the esplanade was stuck with purple figs.
The flying boat circled for hours and couldn't land.

That was the week I met Slessor alone
walking down Phillip Street smoking his cigar,
his pink scrubbed skin never touched by the sun.
Fastidious, bow tie, he smiled like the Cheshire cat:
"If you change your city you are sure to change your
   style."
A kind man, he always praised the young.

IL CONVENTO, BATIGNANO
for Robert Brain

Awake at dawn the garden drew me down,
soft pink touching the Tuscan hills,
to see the paths and channels you had made.
An early tortoise hobbled on the lawn.

Everybody sleeping. I could see
the town below, the cemetery's white wall,
and hear dogs barking in a distant cage.
You said, "You'll find the place is still a mess".

"It's work on hand, progress, bricks, cement.
You can't restore a ruin in a year,
and I'm not Martin Boyd or Henry James."
You laughed and said, "I bet you wish you were".

The lives unlived, the roads we didn't take,
the steady incompletion of our days.
You belong to more worlds than I know,
at home in several countries, caught in none.

Late in the day we fill in twenty years
when paths decided led us different ways:
"I could have been the last expatriate,
mine is poetry for those who don't belong."
"Somehow I feel everywhere at home."

You stretch and realign a damaged frond
and as we talk the chirr and whirr begin
and bees come down like cattle to the pond.

THE TRAVELLER RETURNS

We do not know if gods preside
but I believe in angels seeing clouds
pierced by rays through pencilled distant slopes.
After slow cathedrals, pilgrim towns
Sydney's violent sky can offer this

moment that catches us still unprepared.

Murillo's dark madonna knew such cloud.

Watching the Pacific lick its samples of gold leaf
I voice once more my disbelief aloud.

THE MAN FERN NEAR THE BUS STOP

The man fern near the bus stop waves at me
one scaly feather swaying out of the dark,
slightly drunk with rain and freckled with old spores
it touches me with its slow question mark.

Something in the shadows catches at the throat,
smelling like old slippers, drying like a skin,
scraped like an emu or a gumboot stuck with fur,
straining all the time to take me in.

Cellophane crinkles in the fern's pineapple heart.
The fur parts slowly showing a crumpled horn.
A ruffled seahorse stands in swaying weed,
and held in cotton wool, a mouse unborn.

I look down at it now, a tiny toe, a crook,
remembering voices and growth without choice —
the buds of fingers breaking into power
and long fibres breaking in the voice.

From
TIDE COUNTRY
with new poems

ONION IN A JAR

First week and then a few white threads appear
letting out ends like a cut ball of string,
tentative endeavour of the touching roots to swim,
tentacles that neither breed nor sting.

And slowly too probing towards the top
from the dead crater thrusts a thumb of green,
a mutant antler or a stalk of eye —
the health of ponds where all new growth is clean.

MY MORNING DIP

These are the years when some will change their style
and others cease to write to build a garden,
when the academic starts to grow stiff joints
and the hack's arteries begin to harden

when marriages break up or settle down
some at last embrace their long-lost cause,
while others change their sex or flounder through
the menopause.

And I am trying just to keep afloat
(I can't believe the weather will get finer)
with much to remember, nothing to forget:

Arthur Waley never went to China

and I'll not grow a pony tail
or join a commune yet.

THE EDGE OF WINTER

Ferocity of parrots driven down
by early mountain snow to haunt our bay:
they tear apart the coral's crested flowers
to suck the sugars and the juice all day.

Such images of hunger strike our lives
the way that summer lightning rips the sky;
they scream and swoop and scatter flowers among
the other flowers they break with swivelled tongue —
like green velvet with unbuttoned eye.

Remember all that rain five years ago?
Books bred fungus, each wall its stain.
Our lives were kept indoors like animals
while boredom ate the protein in the brain.

And then one day the rain began to lift.
We went outside recalling summer skies.
The letterbox half hanging from its hinge
was full of drowned and broken butterflies.

STILL LIFE

This still life is still life after all.
These massed hydrangeas standing near the wall
as big as cushions puffed up on a chair
loll their heads like pink clowns in the air
who just perform and do not need to know.
They bloom with blue like heaped-up mountain snow.

These flowers bring such fullness to the room
they stand like resurrections from the tomb.
Now at season's end with tarnished golds
the year rots like a mirror which still holds
blue and silver merging with the frame.
These are colours with a flower's name.

We sit and watch their clouds of pink, their sheen,
the way they look both savage and serene
drawing the light and holding it at bay:
a storm inside a storm that has been stilled
with something finished, something unfulfilled.

THE RESTORERS

I read in today's paper how the scrub
is getting help from its new band of friends:
regeneration of depleted park,

forest will recover lost growth;
the Big Scrub logged away by '99
now furnished with a thousand tiny trees.

And suddenly the names all come alive,
wildings planted out in the thin rain,
white cedar, cheesewood, yellow wood, black bean

lifting their leaves from earth's torn tapestry.
And I remember nuns before the war
with needles into lace restoring threads

bringing back to life a lost design.

REVISITING

Visiting the suburbs of my youth,
a tourist in the town where I was born,
I sit on the new steps in the cold sun

remembering the trees, the rough lawn
sloping slowly down towards the wharves.
You can't go home again the novel claimed —

not with the house erased, the garden gone
although still undemolished in my mind,
and still intact the white picket fence.

We can't rewrite the past to suit our needs
though some will fake their lives to fit their poems.
The present is a concrete path with weeds.

The picture in my mind records each change
with minute details showing what has gone
and everywhere the sky, the mountain range.

The corner grocer's now an antique shop
with etchings in the window showing grasses
in lines that live and touch with small shocks.

Against the hard step a patch of sun
dries unblown seeds on dandelion clocks
swaying the way the breeze moves as it passes.

THE TOWER
Muzot

What was it drove us on that summer day
past the long fields and slopes spread out with hay,
the road with vines, and sheds that smelt of cows
and the warm brooding heaviness of dung —
was it an impulse that he too had sung?

Years ago we felt his gentle power,
reading the book that showed this martial tower,
its reconverted chapel and its trees.
But photos always simplify a scene;
this cannot be the way it would have been
across the road from service station, bar,
a half-deserted café with no name
and stickers for the tourist and his car
and all the life that flourishes on fame.

And yet how private still
the moment we step through the garden wall
and walk towards the well-lit narrow rooms
to see his writing table and his bed.
The house contains a peace we can't define
as if we really could speak to the dead
beyond the forced allusions of a shrine.

LATE MAY: SYDNEY

Autumn in the tropics: even here
the first touch of winter clears the air
making the light astringent and serene.

The coral-trees begin to lose their leaves
letting through the huge waste of the sky;
the scarlet spikes already start to flower.

Morning sun finds shadows grey and blue —
the granite blue of pigeons on the beach
abandoned to their picking and the gulls.

The spider lifts its way beneath the leaf
and we find our contentment talking here
of people and the games words like to play.

Stevenson called Sydney the New South Pole
and played a penny whistle when it rained.
He heard the palm trees squeaking in the square.

Lawrence thought Sydney was innocent and clean,
unready still, but sure to have its day ...
Perhaps this is it we smile and do not say.

LOOKING BACK

We never had the money or the land
we lived in rented rooms
from day to day
from hand to hand
we knew the gifts that still arise unplanned

we were never mainstream anyway
we had no background past a weekly pay
and then the dole and then a pension of a kind
and though things were not right we were not wronged
we learned how not to mind
we never belonged

peripheries at most times were our line
living on the outskirts half the time
or down a lane
my father said, "Don't read too much
it will affect your brain".

our vegetables were grown in backyard lots
my mother grew her flowers in old pots
and trees in kerosene tins near the door

we were what you call the urban poor

DUNG BEETLES

No wonder ancient Egypt worshipped them,
swift, efficient, frugal, patient, clean:
I watch them treat a dog's turd on the lawn
with rites unfolding neatly as a screen.
They love their work, they live on what they do.

How energetic all their efforts seem,
point and persistence, action and routine,
clearing a space, concealing underground
the dreck that unconsumed becomes obscene;
and so they dig and so they raise a mound.

Tenacity and quietness, such calm
lacquered undertakers, rubbish men,
your little squad comes in and you dispose.
A sense of purpose drives your silent look.
I give you pride of place in my new book
of emblems with the eagle and the rose.

TASMANIA

Watercolour country. Here the hills
rot like rugs beneath enormous skies
and all day long the shadows of the clouds
stain the paddocks with their running dyes.

In the small valleys and along the coast,
the land untamed between the scattered farms,
deconsecrated churches lose their paint
and failing pubs their fading coats of arms.

Beyond the beach the pine trees creak and moan,
in the long valley poplars in a row,
the hills breathing like a horse's flank
with grasses combed and clean of the last snow.

AUTUMN READING

Carlyle's *Life of Sterling:* what a book!
The Nicol Stenhouse copy that I read
is dated Sydney 1852:
a book, a life, a destiny, a deed.

I've reached the years where I prefer the past
and its achievements — houses, books and stones —
things that survived and will survive my life
now I've more time behind me than ahead.

How tenderly Carlyle writes about his friend
and all their promise coming into leaf:
they shared Augustine's love of things that weren't
themselves: learning, scholarship and art
and ways to live the good life to the end.

I read this volume in the tropic zone
with late autumn thunder, purple skies.
The palm trees swing and clatter in the breeze
as Sterling in the Indies rides a storm —
a book that passed through many different hands,
a work that has endured and found its place.

We're much less certain now of what will last,
we know how mutable is reputation.
Carlyle did not waver in his view.
But even as the sky grumbles and palms sway
and Sterling cannot win against his illness
I read a voice that utters to our needs,
"Absorb and grow and find your central stillness".

CONVOLVULUS

The tendrils shoot towards us through the green
of plums and lemons wearing a shawl of leaves.
We drag at a single twine and the vine
trembles and the whole garden heaves.

A liquid latticework alive as eels —
less than a week to rope the ficus in.
It celebrates with flags and festoons
and waits for the next foray to begin.

Each flower opens from its chrysalis
such tiny trumpets twirling on their stems,
liqueur glasses balanced on the air,
flaring for bees, dreaming stratagems.

This is the time when nature starts to move
tangling with neglect and with repose.
The leaves are spreading like a waterfall.
They have designs on us and on the rose.

AT THE PARROT HOUSE, TARONGA PARK

What images could yet suggest their range
of tender colours, thick as old brocade,
or shot silk or flowers on a dress
where black and rose and lime seem to caress
the red that starts to shimmer as they fade?

Like something half remembered from a dream
they come from places we have never seen.

They chatter and they squawk and sometimes scream.

Here the macaw clings at the rings to show
the young galahs talking as they feed
with feathers soft and pink as dawn on snow
that it too has a dry and dusky tongue.
Their murmuring embraces every need
from languid vanity to wildest greed.

In the far corner sit two smoky crones
their heads together in a kind of love.
One cleans the other's feathers while it moans.
The others seem to whisper behind fans
while noble dandies gamble in a room
asserting values everyone rejects.

A lidded eye observes, and it reflects.

The peacocks still pretend they own the yard.

For all the softness, how the beaks are hard.

FROM KOREA

A cuckoo in Korea called me out
towards the forest near the new hotel,
the light of dawn still tender on the trees.
I heard the bird quite close I couldn't see.

The garden looked alive, alone, itself —
pines propped on crutches, lichen healing stones,
and water in a pool that plopped and flopped.

The Silla hills of Kyongui at dawn,
the clipped grass of ancient tumuli —
we need such conversations with the dead,
or if not conversations presences,
the sense of clear proportions cut in stone.

Sokkuram's Buddha calls its pilgrims up
the long path that leads into its cave
and has done so for fourteen hundred years.
The apostles could be Gothic effigies.
We look at them through glass among the crowds
who come as tourists not as the devout.

Some are born to faith and fixed belief,
some are born to wander and observe,
and some revere what never can be known.

These hills are older than the tombs they hold,
more ancient than the temples, trees and grass.
The spark of life cannot be held in stone.

The cuckoo keeps its call up in the trees
a moment longer as the day begins
with harder light and lorries on the road.

CHANCE MEETING

My last day in Paris, so I stroll
along the boulevards, through the arcades.
The sun shines, but ice is in the air.

Austerity and uniformity
and last leaves clinging to their trees.
Browsing along the quay I see your book

a neat translation waiting on a tray,
a French remainder, decades out of print.
How tickled you would be to see it here.
I stop and turn the pages, turn away.

Such threads and lines that link our different lives,
coincidence or miracle, who knows
what random purpose conjures and contrives?
Along the street a cold wind blows.

How you would gosh to know I found you here
in Paris where the angels bless and smile:
"I want my books to keep my name alive
if they can keep me living for a while.
I must believe that everything will hold.
I've always known the glitter from the gold".

We often wondered what controls our lives,
if unseen presences surround, attend;
our notions of the afterlife weren't clear.
But as I walked the windy street, old friend,
you were alive again and strangely near.

SPARROWS: MOSMAN

Sparrows in bamboo: a thousand birds
or near enough to judge from all their noise.
They've made the corner garden a dry room,
a gambling den, a marketplace, a pad.
Word gets around, the messages are clear,
the day is coming they will have to go.

Such chirruping, such twittering, such flit.
They need the mild evening or dawn
light as shrill cicadas need the sun.
How ravishing their clamour as they cling
and amplify their hard and grainy sound,
the music of their airy scampering.

An artist from Japan would get this right
in two ticks showing nature's life
simply doesn't need us to go on:
a stone wall, a clutter of bamboo —
a few lines that gather up the whole
the way a tendril speaks for the full vine,
a brushstroke sparrow for a thousand birds.

And here I sit and listen to their din
and how they turn the garden to a room.

POETRY READING

A lunchtime reading, in the crypt, St Paul's;
a grey day with pigeons on the lawn
and memories of Donne and the divines.
The audience informal, some forlorn,

until we hear the tapping of a stick
and the dean leads the poet to a chair:
a short introduction (life and works)
and the real reason (beaming) we are here.

The poet smooths the lectern with his hand;
there is a drawn-out silence of a kind
hovering on the edge of awkwardness,
and as he speaks, I see that he is blind,

a fact so clear it doesn't rate a mention.
His poems are a cycle about birds,
seen once and remembered, I can't tell,
and how they live within his world of words:

a sparrow picking near a rubbish tip
and quail too plump to run far or to fly,
the Alexandrian ibises he knew,
finding their noble pathway through the sky.

And then you read your "little bestiary"
and tapped a tortoise with your fingertips
and what we saw hobbling across the floor
was conjured up from sounds behind your lips.

You seemed to write each poem as you spoke.
I heard your patience and your skill define
a pair of herons treading through the grass
with purpose and with vision both in line.

IN THE COLONIAL MUSEUM
to the memory of Louisa Anne Meredith (1812–1895)

The world that you belonged to is no more;
perhaps that's why we care for it so much.
You had the time to tinker and retouch,
to patch and mend, recover and restore,
and things grew old as slowly as a face,
secure as the hanging of a door.

The arts and crafts that took up time —
scrimshaw, lacework, painting, cameo —
depict a world that we no longer know
like garden paths with wild columbine.
And objects had a simple tale to tell
like poems that were written well.

A paint box rests on velvet under glass:
the hollow squares of colour start to fade.
Your sketchbook opens at the final page
showing a cow, a lake, a clump of grass
and in the corner doodled native flowers,
and this was just the margin of your life,
the way you spent what you called your spare hours.

And in between came the unending chores,
the needs of others and the daily tasks,
trimming the lamp and polishing the floors
and what it must have cost nobody asks,
but life was lived with fortitude and grace.
And things endured. And here they rest in place.

TRANSLATIONS AND VARIATIONS

DELIE, OBIECT DE PLVS HAVLTE VERTU (1544)
after Maurice Scève

i
Without harm the Royal Serpent lives
within its burning element, the flame;
and my desire that your look revives
delights you from the distance that you claim,
and though you know, though fire hurt and maim,
yet you delight in it — your element.
 O that you were (indifferent and cold)
the salamander living in my fire:
you'd find there everything you'd ever need
and eat away my tender harsh desire
and satisfy my longing's gentle greed.

ii
Nothing or very little is required
to separate me from this mortal home:
to which the spirit consents. Its long-desired
immortality it sees will come.
Dying is only death for a short while.
 And thus I shall not fear to be reborn
out of my death into all peace, a soul.
The day begins to die, yet it is morn.
Evening here means dawn at the other pole.

VARIATIONS ON GARNIER'S PERPETUUM MOBILE

1
The moon
isn't it like our poetry
so dead
so clear.

2
Stones are neither hungry nor thirsty

Only our flesh
hungers
for stones.

3
Bird
consumes itself
in bird

There are cries in the sky.

4
One must distinguish
the voice of the sea
which is breakings and rumours

and the voice of the mountain

which fills space
without a fold.

SUMMER FEELING
after Britting

Short summer, glowing, remain. Though your breath
disturbs the anxious grass, the corn
loves you, and the ripening wine.
The cricket sings your song of praise.

And the lark, when it climbs in the blue,
does so with a trill to please you,
and the wild poppy's scarlet flower
is a fiery cry of jubilation.

In the cool, glittering nights
the grass stands up once more,
the snail wanders through the dew-wet land
and does not see the stars above

beyond the reach of its feelers.
It is already afraid like the toad in its black hole,
like the salamander in the swamp
of the sweet and rosy morning.

CROWS IN WINTER
after Britting

They've come at last these wild crows,
the snow is heaped both fresh and hard,
to sit upon the silent tree
that drew the wind into the yard.

Magic birds from long ago
why have you come to visit me,
wearing still your gallow clothes?
Once you knew the hangman's tree.

But no; I see you merely stare
alone, ahead. There is no sun.
The sky is grey and without shape:
so was the world when just begun.

And from the stones another bird
flaps to the tree and shakes, ignored,
his shabby, cracked, and tired wings:
he's angry, full of spite and bored:

and through the winter calm there runs
his shallow, broken, strident cry.
Heraldic birds and birds of dreams,
strips of rock and storm-filled sky,

they stare and crouch, indifferent;
their eyes are deadened with distrust.
The new snow falls and spirals down
gently falling — where it must.

UNDER THE PINE
after Peter Huchel

Needles without eyes
the fog draws
the white threads in.
Fish bones
scraped into the sand.
With cat's paws
the ivy
climbs
the trunk.

HOUSE FOR SALE
after André Frénaud

So many people have lived here who loved
love, awakening and sweeping up the dust.
The well is bottomless and doesn't show the moon,
the ancients have gone and taken nothing away.
The ivy takes over beneath the winter sky,
and only soot remains, their mark of coffee grounds.
I settle down now to long unravelled dreams.
I love the scum of other people's souls
mixed with the garnet-coloured fringes of the chairs,
the greasy dirt of failed enterprises.
Concierge, I'll buy, I'll buy the wretched wreck.
If it poisons me I'll go up in flames with it.
We will open the windows ... Put up the plate.
A man enters, sniffs, and starts all over again.

POEMS AFTER PAUL CELAN

CORONA

Out of my hand autumn eats its leaf: we are friends.
We shell time from the nuts and teach it to walk;
time goes back into its shell.

In the mirror it is Sunday,
in the dream there is sleeping,
the mouth speaks the truth.

My eye descends to the sex of my loved one:
we look at each other,
we whisper darkness to each other,
we love each other like poppy and memory,
we sleep like wine in the sea-shells,
like the sea in the ray of blood of the moon.

We stand entwined in the window, they watch us from
    the street:
it is time that people knew.
It is time the stone condescended to bloom,
that unrest inspired a heart to beat.
It is time that it became time.

It is time.

FLOWER

The stone.
The stone in the air that I followed.
Your eye as blind as the stone.

We were
hands,
we scooped out the darkness, we found
the word which came up along the summer:
flower.

Flower — a word for the blind.
Your eye and my eye:
they supply
water.

Growth.
Heartwell by heart wall
puts forth new leaves.

One word more, like this, and the hammers
swing in the open.

IN PRAISE OF DISTANCE

In the spring of your eyes
live the nets of the fishermen of the mad sea.
In the spring of your eyes
the sea keeps its promises.

Here I, a heart
that has dwelt among humans,
cast off my clothes and the lustre of an oath:

blacker in black, I am more naked.
Only now disloyal am I faithful.
I am you when I am I

in the spring of your eyes
I drift and dream of plunder.

A net catches a net
we part embracing.

In the spring of your eyes
a hanged man strangles the rope.

MENHIR

Growing
form of grey
eyeless one
stone gaze
through you
earth moves towards us
human
on dark and white heath paths
at evening
in front of you
heaven's ravine.

Botched, discarded, sunken
over the heart's crest grinding
millstones of the sea.

Bright-flighted you hang early
between gorse and stone
little phallic pillar.

Black, phylactery coloured
so you wait
you pods
who join in our prayers.

WITH CHANGING KEY

With changing key
you unlock the house in which
the snow of unuttered things is blowing.
According to the blood that flows
from your eye or mouth or ear,
your key changes.

If your key changes, the word changes
which is allowed to blow with the flakes.
It depends on the wind which drives you away
what snow hardens around the word.

ICH BIN ALLEIN

I am alone, I put the ash flower
in the glass full of ripe blackness. Sister mouth
you speak a word that lives on outside the windows,
and what I dreamed climbs up me silently.

I stand in the bloom of the withered hour
and save up a drop of resin for a late bird:
it carries a flake of snow on a life-red feather;
the grain of ice in its beak, it will get through the
    summer.

THE WHITEST DOVE OF ALL

The whitest dove of all flew up: I am allowed to love
  you.
In the gentle window sways the gentle door.
The still tree stepped into the still room.
You are as near as if you were not here.

Out of my hand you take the big flower.
It is not white nor red nor blue — but you take it.
Where it never was it will forever stay.
We never were, so we remain with it.

SLEEP THEN

Sleep then and my eye will remain open.
Rain filled the pitcher and we emptied it.
The night will drive a heart, the heart will drive a blade —
But it is too late lady, too late to reap.

Nightwind your hair is snowhite, white!
White what remains to me and white what I lose!
She counts the hours and I count the years.
We drank rain. Rain is what we chose.

SLEEP AND FOOD

The breath of the night is your shroud, the darkness
  lies down with you.
It touches ankle and temple, it wakes you to life and
  sleep,
it finds you out in word and wish and thought,
it sleeps with every one of them, it lures you out.
It combs the salt out of your eyelashes and serves it up
  to you,
and what it was as rose, shadow and water
it pours into you.

I HEARD IT SAID

I heard it said there is
a stone and a circle in the water
and over the water a word
that laid the circle round the stone.

I saw my poplar go down to the water,
I saw how its arm reached down into the deep,
I saw its roots imploring heaven for night.

I did not hurry after it,
I only gathered up from the earth that crumb
which had the shape and nobility of your eye,
I took the chain of maxims from your neck
and hemmed the table with it where the crumb now lay.

And saw my poplar no more.